DATE DUE

NO 2'98		
MR 1'99		
DE 18'99		
AG 5'00		
JY 30'01		
JE 3'04		

HAPPY BIRTHDAYS
ROUND THE WORLD

Chicago · New York · San Francisco

HAPPY BIRTHDAYS
OUND THE WORLD

by Lois S. Johnson

illustrated by Genia

 RAND McNALLY & COMPANY

Republished by Omnigraphics ● Penobscot Building ● Detroit ● 1993

happy birthday wishes to
my friendly sister,
Frances V. Smith
and to my sisterly friend,
Helen V. Monegan

Library of Congress Cataloging-in-Publication Data

Johnson, Lois S.
 Happy birthdays round the world / Lois S. Johnson ; illustrated by
Genia.
  p. cm.
 Originally published: New York : Rand McNally, 1963.
 Includes index.
 Summary: Describes birthday party customs from twenty-four
different countries.
  ISBN 1-55888-174-3 (lib. bdg. : acid-free paper)
  1. Birthdays. [1. Birthdays.] I. Title.
GT2430.J64 1993
394.2—dc20   93-24339
                                                       CIP
                                                        AC

This book is printed on acid free paper meeting the ANSI Z39.48 Standard. The
infinity symbol that appears above indicates that the paper in this book meets
that standard.

Printed in the United States of America

CONTENTS

INTRODUCTION: ONCE UPON
A BIRTHDAY

⸺ Once upon a birthday, when early people had no way of marking time except by the moon or by some important event, little attention was paid to the anniversary of a person's birth. Everyone knew, of course, that people grew older as time passed, but they marked no special milestone.

As people progressed and learned more about the passage of time, they began to note time changes. A calendar was invented. Anniversaries became important, and special celebrations grew up around birthdays.

Stories from the Old Testament tell of some of the early birthday celebrations.

We read in the Bible that King Pharaoh celebrated his birthday by making a feast for his court followers. That was over 4,000 years ago. The story of wicked King Herod tells that on his birthday he "made a supper to his lords, high captains," and other special friends in Galilee. At this feast Herod provided dancing girls to entertain his guests.

The Bible story that we know best is the one about the birth of the Christ Child in Bethlehem.

For nearly 2,000 years since that day, the Christian world has kept the anniversary of this birth. That celebration is, of course, Christmas.

Early birthday observances were held only to honor prominent men in a country. Little attention was paid to the birthdays of common people, and practically none was given to those of children.

Today children in many countries round the world celebrate their birthdays. Sometimes their customs differ from ours, but they all enjoy their special days in their own way.

In some countries children generally celebrate their saints' name days each year instead of their own birthdays. Parents in those countries follow an old custom of giving the name of a saint to their child when he is baptized. This saint becomes the child's guardian or patron saint throughout his lifetime. To show special honor to his saint, the child celebrates the day each year that has been declared sacred to the saint. For instance, if a girl is named Agnes in honor of St. Agnes, the Martyr, she will celebrate on January 21st, which is the name day of this saint. A boy with the name of Francis Xavier will celebrate on December 3rd, St. Francis Xavier Day.

This special day is known in some countries as Saint's Day, and as Name Day in others. It does not matter which word is used, for the idea is the same. Besides observing his saint's day, in some countries a child may be lucky enough to celebrate on his own birthday, too, having two celebrations in one year.

Since it was not possible to include all countries of the world in this book, I tried, first, to give a global picture by including countries in the Western Hemisphere, Europe, the Middle East, Africa, Asia, and the Far East.

From these areas, I then chose the countries in which birthday customs usually differ from those in the United States. (Children in Austria, Denmark, Ireland, Sweden, and Switzerland, for example, celebrate their birthdays very much as you do.)

Birthday and name-day customs described are not always typical of the entire country. All customs are affected in all countries by differences in language, religion, geographic location (rural, urban, regional), and economic status. But the customs are, so far as I have been able to find out, followed by the majority of people in each country. Even in the United States, not all children have parties, or birthday cakes with candles, but most of them do.

Many of the costumes shown in the illustrations are used only at festival time; some of them are worn in one part of the country, but not in another. Costumes differ for the same reasons that customs do.

Although customs differ from country to country, there are also many similarities. I hope you will find it interesting to discover that even with their differences, people everywhere are also much alike.

LOIS S. JOHNSON

Part One

BIRTHDAY CUSTOMS AND
HOW THEY GREW

Parties, Presents,
and Good Wishes

⌒⌒ The custom of giving parties on birthdays goes
back to the days when people believed that good
and evil spirits, sometimes known as good and bad
fairies, appeared at the time of a child's birth and
influenced him all through life. These early people
also believed that any kind of change in a person's
life was a dangerous thing, because then evil spirits
were thought to be especially active. Birthdays were
believed to be filled with unknown dangers because
they marked a time change from one year to another.

In order to keep the evil spirits from working
their harmful black magic at these birthday changes,
people tried to think of ways to protect the one who
was having a birthday.

They then began the custom of giving a birthday party to which they invited friends and members
of the family of the birthday person. They believed

that by surrounding him with good friends and showering him with good wishes, they would scare away the evil spirits so they could not get close enough to do him harm.

The influence for good was considered even more powerful if the well-wishers also presented gifts along with their good wishes. And the earlier in the day that the gifts and greetings were presented, the greater would be the protection from the evil ones, and the more certain it would be that good fortune and a long life would come to the person celebrating.

The Germans are given credit for starting celebrations of children's birthdays. These celebrations are called *kinderfeste*. The word *kinderfest* comes from the two German words, *kinder*, which means "children," and *fest*, which means "festival" or "party."

That was many years ago, but ever since that time, parties have continued to be a part of children's birthday celebrations.

Cakes, Candles, and Magic Wishes

Cakes have long been an important part of special occasions such as Christmas, Easter, weddings, and other festive days. It is not surprising then that cakes became a part of birthday celebrations, too.

Sometimes birthday cakes are used to tell fortunes. A coin, a button, a ring, and a thimble are often placed in the cake dough before it is baked. When the cake is baked and sliced, anyone who finds one of the objects in his slice is supposed to learn what his future will be. It is believed, by the superstitious, that the one who gets the coin will be wealthy, the one who gets the button will be poor, the one who gets the ring will marry some day, and the one who gets the thimble will be an old maid or a bachelor.

The custom of decorating the birthday cake

with lighted candles seems to have been started by the Germans. The Germans adapted an old belief, probably held first by the early Greeks and Romans, that lit tapers or candles had magic qualities. According to stories that have come down to us, these early peoples would light fires on their altars to show their gods how much they respected and honored them. They believed that the prayers they offered would be carried upward to the gods on the rising flames, and that the gods would then send down blessings to them.

The next time you celebrate your birthday and a big cake is set in front of you ablaze with candles—one for each year and one to grow on—you can remember that you are following an old, old superstition.

And when you make a secret wish, and puff out your cheeks so you can blow out the burning candles in one whiff, you are not just trying to impress everyone with your skill at blowing; you are also trying your best to work the magic that will make your wish come true. If even one candle is still burning after your first puff, your wish will not come true, for that is the way the magic has worked for years and years! Of course today no one really believes that, but pretending adds to the fun.

Birthday Games

People used to believe that the beginning of a new game was like the beginning of a new year. In the same way, the end of a game signified the ending of the year just past.

That long-time favorite game for birthday parties, *Pinning the Tail on the Donkey*, may have superstitions connected with it. When a player starts out with a blindfold over his eyes to pin the tail where it is supposed to go, he never knows whether he will hit the right place or not. He keeps stabbing away, hoping all the time to be lucky so the prize will be his. Life, some people used to think, was much like this game. A person starting out on a new

year was like the blindfolded player, because he had no way of knowing whether he would succeed during the coming year, or not! All he knew was that he must try his best and hope that at last he would "hit the right mark."

Another game that many children think is fun, although the one having the birthday may not always agree, is that of giving spanks, one for each year, and then: one to grow on; one to live on; one to eat on; one to be happy on; one to get married on.

This may be harmless fun, but it started as an old superstition hundreds of years ago, when it was considered bad luck if a birthday person were not spanked. According to one early belief, the spanks were supposed to soften up the body for the tomb! Probably this was just someone's idea of a joke and really meant nothing of the kind. Certainly we don't believe it any longer.

Birthday Trees

In some countries a birthday tree is planted on the day a baby is born to bring him good luck all through his life. The tree is tended carefully because its growth is supposed to foretell the way the child will grow. If the tree thrives, the child will thrive also and will have good fortune. If the tree should

be cut down or should wither and die, then the belief is that the child may be injured, become ill, or perhaps die. It is not to be wondered at that people who plant birthday trees for their children consider it very important to take care of them, just as they try to take good care of their children.

This custom is followed today in the country districts of some European countries, especially in Germany. In Switzerland a pear tree is often planted for a girl, an apple tree for a boy.

A Rhyme, Two Sayings, and a Song

A Mother Goose rhyme that has been a favorite among children for many, many years, is this one about birthdays:

> *Monday's child is fair of face,*
> *Tuesday's child is full of grace,*
> *Wednesday's child is sour and sad,*
> *Thursday's child is merry and glad,*
> *Friday's child is loving and giving,*
> *Saturday's child must work for a living,*
> *While the child that is born on the Sabbath*
> *   Day,*
> *Is blithe and bonny and good and gay.*

So, if you are superstitious, just ask your mother on what day of the week you were born, and you will know what kind of a person you are!

Two sayings that have been repeated by children as far back as anyone can remember are these: "If you cry on your birthday you will cry every day of the coming year," and "The seventh child of a seventh child will be brilliant and become famous."

Music has always played a part in celebrations and festivals. Birthdays have special songs in many countries. Some of these songs express the love and admiration the singers have for the person celebrating his special day. Others express good wishes for health, happiness, and long life. All are filled with the spirit of joy and friendship.

Even though some countries may have their own traditional birthday songs, the one birthday song that is becoming most popular all around the world is the American favorite:

> *Happy birthday to you,*
> *Happy birthday to you,*
> *Happy birthday, dear (name),*
> *Happy birthday to you.*

This song was written many years ago by Mildred J. and Patty S. Hill. No one seems to know exactly when it was written, but it is probably more than 60 years old. Like many folk songs, it has been passed on by one person's singing it to another, until today the singing of *Happy Birthday* has spread all over the world.

We like to think the Happy Birthday song is a tradition that American children have given to children of other countries. As it is, American children owe a big "thank you" to many countries for their own well-loved birthday traditions, because it was the early settlers of the United States who brought with them their old-world customs of birthday celebrations. It is nice to think, in return, that the birthday song, as well as some of the other favorite American birthday customs, can be shared with children of other countries.

BIRTHDAYS, NAME DAYS, OR SAINTS' DAYS

In Belgium

⁓ Belgium is a small country but a beautiful one, full of traditions, and its inhabitants are warm and friendly. About half the people in Belgium speak French, the other half, Flemish, although many use both languages. Those who live in the south would be greeted on their birthday morning with a cheery *Joyeux Anniversaire*, which is French; those who live in the north would be wished a *Gelukkige Verjaardag*, which is Flemish.

There was a time when Belgian boys and girls celebrated their saints' days, but this custom is giving way to birthday celebrations.

Today they enjoy birthday parties, much as the children in the United States do. They like their birthday cake and candles. They give one another gifts, and are beginning the custom of sending cards of greetings. Sometimes a birthday dinner is given, when close relatives and friends are invited.

Belgian children have a favorite birthday song of their own which they enjoy singing at their parties. In French, the words are:

Bon anniversaire,
Nos voeux les plus sincères,
Que ces quelques fleurs
Vous apportent le bonheur,
Que la vie entière
Vous soit douce et légère
Et que l'an prochain
Nous soyons tous réunis
Pour chanter en choeur,
"Bon anniversaire."

Translated into English, the words mean:

Happy birthday,
Our most sincere wishes
That these few flowers
We bring to you
May bring you happiness,
That your whole life long
May be pleasant and free from care,
And that next year
Will see us reunited
To sing in chorus for you,
"Happy birthday!"

Joyeux Anniversaire—zhwah *-yehs* a-nee-ver-*sare*

Gelukkige Verjaardag—geh-*look*-keeg-ah vehr-*yahr*-dahg

In Brazil

Feliz Aniversário, Feliz Aniversário, (Happy Birthday, Happy Birthday) is the Portuguese good wish that greets a Brazilian boy or girl on his birthday. If you should ask him why the greeting is in Portuguese instead of in Spanish, when all of the other people of South America speak Spanish, the Brazilian would tell you proudly that his language and many of his customs come from his Portuguese ancestors who settled Brazil after the Portuguese Admiral Pedro Alvaro Cabral had discovered it in 1500.

Brazilian children would tell you, too, that birthdays are considered big events in their lives. A mother will plan well ahead of the day to make the birthday party for her child something very special. She will spend days baking cakes and cookies, and even more time making many kinds of fancy candies for the event. Candies are a specialty of the Brazilians, and a birthday party must of course have the finest and the most elaborate candies a mother can make.

When the guests arrive for the party, they first have fun singing together, dancing, and playing games. Then the mother invites everyone to the birthday table—and the party really begins!

The table is decorated with bowls of bright colored flowers and gay paper festoons. Up and down the length of the tables, plates have been set, which are piled high with the special birthday candies. Some of the candies—molded and colored fondant in the shapes of strawberries, cherries, tomatoes, bananas, and other kinds of fruit—look almost too real and too pretty to eat. Other candies are a mixture of pineapple, coconut, nuts, and fondant, shaped into delicious balls. Big juicy prunes, stuffed with coconut and nuts, are still another tempting sweet.

After the children have taken their seats at the table, dishes of ice cream are brought, and the plates of candies passed. Then an elaborately decorated cake, alight with candles, is set before the honored birthday child to make a wish on, and to cut for sharing with his friends.

As the cake is brought, the children all sing in Portuguese *Happy Birthday to You:*

> *Feliz aniversário para você,*
> *Feliz aniversário para (name)*
> *Muita felicidade para você,*
> *Muitos anos de vida.*

The English meaning of the words in the first two lines of the song can almost be guessed:

Happy birthday to you,
Happy birthday to (name)—

The last two lines, however, are somewhat different from the familiar words:

Lots of happiness to you,
Many years of life.

The most important birthday of all in Brazil is a girl's fifteenth birthday. A big party is often held in honor of this occasion, to which young men and boys may be invited. They would feel insulted, however, should anyone suggest that a birthday party be given in their honor!

But to a Brazilian girl, this party is the most important thing she has ever had happen to her, and is an event she has long been dreaming about. The affair is much like the coming-out parties in this country. Parents take pride in presenting their beautiful daughter to their friends.

Often these parties are dinner-dances at which elaborate buffets are served—baked ham, roast beef, chicken, salads, or a very special treat of roast turkey. With the turkey will be served a delicious dish, called *farofa,* which is a concoction of toasted white coarse flour mixed with butter, seasonings, chopped hard-boiled eggs, onions, raisins, prunes, and parsley.

For dessert on this special occasion, nothing can quite compare with the favorite Brazilian delicacy, *fios de ovo,* or "threads of eggs." Only the most skilled cooks will attempt to make it, for it will never turn out right unless the yolks of the eggs are beaten to the proper lightness, and the temperature of the sirup into which the egg froth is spooned is neither too hot nor too cold. As the froth is lifted from the sirup, it spins long threads. These *fios de ovo* are then carefully lifted into a bowl, and brought to the birthday table to be admired and enjoyed to the last thread.

---

farofa—fah-*roh*-fah

feliz aniversário para você—feh-*lees* ah-nee-vehr-*sah*-ree-oh pah-rah voh-*ceh*

fios de ovo—*fee*-ohse deh *oh*-voh

In Ceylon

Off the southeast coast of India lies the island country of Ceylon, land of tropical palm groves, rice fields, and tea and rubber plantations. It is a land of bright, happy children who love to play together and to celebrate their birthdays.

The first birthday celebration comes when a Ceylonese baby is thirty-one days old. Although he is too young to realize what is going on, his older brothers and sisters, his parents, and their friends make much of the occasion.

Early in the morning the baby is dressed in new clothes and gotten ready for the day. His house is given a thorough cleaning, and incense is burned to purify the air. A priest is usually invited to come to the house to perform religious rites and to give the baby a blessing.

After the service, the family and friends gather for lunch. According to their religious beliefs, no meat is served at this meal—only a variety of fresh vegetables, rice and curry, and milk.

It is the custom in Ceylon, when this first celebration takes place, for a close relative of the family to bring the baby a special gift. For a boy baby, this gift may be a gold chain; for a girl, gold arm bangles.

The parents also present the new baby with a charm, made of copper in a scroll design, which is rolled into a gold-enclosed cylinder or tube. This charm is worn all through the person's life and is supposed to protect him from harm.

Precious jewels are abundant in Ceylon, and are often presented as gifts on birthdays, at the Festival of the Lamps, or on other important occasions. These jewels may be rubies, star sapphires, pearls, topazes—whatever strikes the fancy of the giver and fits the size of his purse. The jewels are usually mounted in rings, bracelets, necklaces, or bangles. They are prized possessions.

On the day of the birthday, friends and relatives come to call to extend their good wishes, and to leave gifts. For children, these gifts may be books, chocolates, sweet biscuits, fancy pins and other jeweled ornaments, or scarves. The parents also present jewels, set in special ways, to their daughters, and new clothes to their sons.

The parents invite their children's friends to help them celebrate at a party during the afternoon of the birthday. They often serve the guests chicken curry, seafood, hard-boiled eggs cooked in coconut

milk, a variety of vegetables and, for dessert, bananas, sugar cane, and cookies. Sometimes a birthday cake with candles will be added.

Christian missionaries were the first to introduce the custom of "western-type" birthday parties. So popular has this new custom become, that even children who are not Christians often persuade their parents to give them parties with a cake and candles, too. These familiar customs of celebrating are fast being adopted in many parts of Ceylon. Children especially enjoy singing "Happy Birthday," sometimes in their own language, sometimes in English.

In China

According to an ancient Chinese custom, everyone adds a year to his age on the Chinese New Year. This day is more important than the anniversary of a person's birth. Since the date for the Chinese New Year is figured according to the phase of the moon, it does not come on January 1 each year as New Year's Day does in other parts of the world.

A baby's birthday is celebrated in China when he is thirty days old and when he is a year old. Then there are no celebrations until the tenth birthday. After that, every tenth year is celebrated for as long as the person lives. The most important date is the thirtieth anniversary, when a child becomes an adult. A big celebration is usually held on this date. The older a person becomes in China, the more elaborate is the birthday celebration. Those who reach their sixtieth or seventieth birthdays are considered to be "Venerable Ones" and are held in great respect.

Children in China do not resent having their birthdays passed over lightly while they are growing up, while so much attention is paid to the anniversaries of the older members of the family. From the moment they can understand anything, they are taught to consider the wishes and pleasures of their elders before their own. This great respect for the older ones of the family is called filial piety.

Chinese boys and girls enjoy the celebrations for their parents and their grandparents and it is also a great day for the brothers and sisters when the baby of the family has his first-month celebration. They are as proud as can be to show off their baby to all the relatives and friends who come to offer congratulations.

Each visitor brings the baby a gift of brightly colored eggs. In return, the parents present eggs to the guests. Some of the eggs—which of course are hard-boiled!—are painted a brilliant red, the favorite color of the Chinese, because it is the symbol of life, fire, and joy. Other eggs may be decorated in delicate designs of many colors. In addition, good luck pieces, charms, necklaces, or lockets are brought to the new baby.

The charms may be made of gold or silver, and are often pinned to the baby's clothes. Good luck pieces in the form of a tiger are the most popular. Chinese children know that the tiger is king of the animals because he fights all the beasts that roam in the forest. He is the symbol of strength and courage, and a tiger's likeness on a charm means that the giver hopes the baby will grow up to be as strong and as brave as a tiger.

A gold necklace, on which is hung a gold charm in the shape of a lock, is another popular gift for a month-old baby. It is believed that so long as a child wears the necklace, the lock will keep away all the harmful influences that may come near.

After the eggs, the charms, and other gifts have been admired, the parents invite their visitors to eat with them in the baby's honor.

On a baby's first birthday, his parents dress him in brightly colored new clothes, which are often of silk. Red, green, and blue are favorite colors. A little round cap, the color of the other clothes, is part of his costume. It is often embroidered in gold or silver thread in the design of a tiger. The baby's new shoes sometimes have a tiger head embroidered on the tips of the toes.

Dressed in his new birthday finery, the baby is then set down by his mother in the middle of a table, upon which she has placed many objects. Children and grown-ups watch to see which object the baby will reach for first, for that, they think will show what his future is to be. Should he reach for a book, he would be a scholar; if he reaches for an abacus, he will go into business. If the baby is a girl, objects for girls would be placed around her,

so that if she picked up a thimble first, she would be skilled in sewing; or if her first choice were a piece of cloth, she would want to wear pretty clothes some day. You may be sure the parents never put objects near the child that would indicate an unhappy future or would show bad luck in any way!

On both of these birthdays, many delicious foods are served—chicken, duck, fish, vegetables, and, for the last course, soup. Noodles are always an important part of a Chinese birthday dinner. Because they are long, they signify long life, and because it takes a great many noodles to fill a bowl, noodles always mean "many happy returns of the day"!

Another custom in China is the serving of special pastries molded and baked in the shape of peaches, then painted red. Since these pastries are really better to look at and admire than to eat, they are usually on trays and set on a table in the center of the room, with candles and burning incense.

These pastries have a special meaning at birthday time.

According to a legend, which Chinese children like to have told to them, there lived, once upon a time, a grand old lady who was said to be immortal. Her home was in the far west in the middle of a great garden in which flourished the strangest and most wonderful trees in the world. The fruit on some of these trees ripened only once in eight hundred years; on others, once in twelve hundred, or even fifteen hundred years. When mortals were lucky enough to eat even so much as one small bite of this magic fruit, it was believed they would live to be at least one hundred years old.

To the Chinese, then, peach-like pastries symbolize the wish for a long life.

And the longer a Chinese lives, the more important do his birthdays become! To the Chinese, the wish for a "long life" has real meaning.

In Germany

When Germans started the custom of having a *kinderfest* to celebrate a child's birthday, they made the child the center of attention on this occasion. The family usually began the day by presenting him with simple gifts that they thought he would like—a ribbon, a toy, a book, or perhaps a pair of warm knitted mittens. The child's mother would let him choose his favorite foods for his birthday dinner. Everyone tried to make him happy all day.

In the afternoon, his mother would let him invite his friends to help him with his *kinderfest* celebration. After playing games or singing songs, the children would be served birthday *kuchen* (cakes) and sweets.

This *kinderfest* custom, begun so many years ago, has continued to be a big part of a German child's birthday celebration, for birthdays are still made much of in Germany.

The birthday usually begins at breakfast time, when the child starts to pull his chair out from under

the table before sitting down to eat. He finds that the seat of his chair has been piled high with packages that his parents and his brothers and sisters have wrapped and placed there for him. He has to open each gift before he can have his breakfast, but this only adds to the excitement of his birthday morning.

Later in the day, he is again honored at a special family dinner. The table is decorated with flowers and is set with the dishes the child likes best. His mother always tries to prepare his favorite foods, too —perhaps, *hasenpfeffer* (rabbit), or *strudel* (pastry), or *kuchen* (cakes).

The best part of the dinner to the child who is celebrating is the elaborately decorated birthday cake, with a circle of burning candles around the edge, one candle for each year and always an extra candle to "grow on." This extra candle is called the "Light of Life."

---

kuchen—*koo*-ken

hasenpfeffer—*hahz*-en-pfef-fer

strudel—*shtroo*-del

kinderfest—*kin*-der-fest

kinderfeste (plural)—*kin*-der-fest-uh

In Ghana

Ghana, a small country along the Gulf of Guinea, on the west coast of Africa, was formerly called the Gold Coast. This nickname was well chosen, because the country is rich in natural resources—gold and other minerals, diamonds, mahogany and other hardwoods, and cocoa (Ghana leads the world in the production of cocoa).

Ghana became independent in 1957, but still shows the British influence in its official language and in many of its customs.

British and American missionaries came to Ghana about one hundred years ago. They are the ones who introduced birthday celebrations, especially those for children. Before this, little, if any, attention was paid to anniversaries. Today birthday celebrations are popular among most of the people.

The missionaries put the native languages into writing and taught the natives how to read. They also gave them a birthday song when they introduced the idea of birthday celebrations.

In the Ev-é dialect, one of the six main languages in Ghana, the words of the birthday song are these:

> *Dzigbe fe yayra netu wò,*
> *Agbe nede agbe dzi na wò,*
> *Fe neva fe dzi na wò,*
> *Mawu neyra wò.*

The words are different from those in our Happy Birthday song, but the same good wishes are expressed.

> *May birthday's blessing be yours,*
> *May many more years be yours,*
> *One year after another,*
> *May God bless you.*

Mother-love is strong in Ghana, and mothers enjoy doing things that will make their children happy. A birthday celebration offers a special opportunity to give their children pleasure.

Usually, the mother invites all her child's friends to a birthday dinner. She works hard to prepare his favorite dishes. The dinner is often held in the late afternoon.

A long table, with benches along each side, is set under the trees, because it is cooler in the shade. A tablecloth is spread over the table, on which the dishes of food are set—perhaps a delicious chicken

stew, rice, hard candies and toffee, and fruit drinks. There may be a cake, but this is not usual.

The children romp and play in the yard after they have had their dinner. They may dress in "western-style" clothes, or may wear their national costume, made of gaily colored prints.

Gifts are not considered important, but eating and playing together are. Children in Ghana are always glad when someone has a birthday and they can wish him: *Dzigbe fe yayra netu wò.*

Dzigbe fe yayra netu wò—*Dzhee*-buhh fuhh yah-*yeer*-ah nuhh-*too* woh

In Great Britain

In merry old Britain, birthday celebrations are made much of. At each anniversary, from the first through the twenty-first, special events mark the day. The fun begins at breakfast time when the family presents its gifts. Then, all during the day, cards and gifts keep arriving from relatives and friends.

At school, from kindergarten through junior high school, each birthday is remembered by the child's teacher with some kind of special ceremony. Sometimes well-meaning classmates may follow the British custom of "bumping." To wish the birthday child well, some of his friends will pick him up by the ankles while others will lift him under the armpits, and then they "bump" him on the ground as many times as he is years old, with, of course, an extra "bump" to grow on.

For the younger children in Great Britain, an afternoon party is planned by the mothers, when friends of the child are invited. Games are played

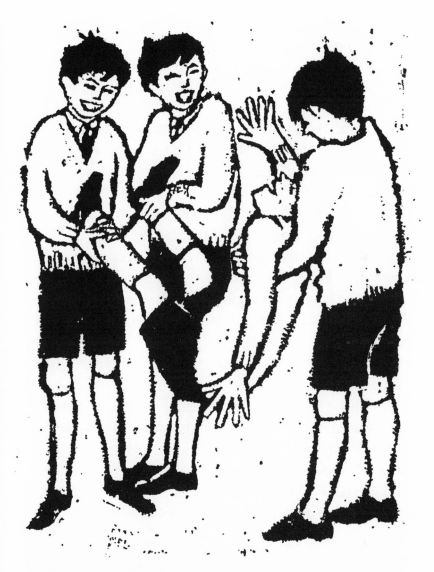

at these parties, and gifts are presented. At tea time
a birthday cake is brought in on a large plate.
Written in icing on top of the cake are the words:
Happy Birthday, Jane (or whatever the child's
name). Birthday candles—one for each year—are

burning on the cake. British children, like American children, are expected to blow out all the candles in one puff so that the coming year will be a happy one. When the birthday child is very small, his mother or father will help to guide his hand while he cuts the first slice of cake. All the little friends join in singing *Happy Birthday to You*.

The most important birthday in Great Britain is the twenty-first, when a person "comes of age." Everyone looks forward to this special occasion.

Relatives and friends shower the twenty-one-year-old all through the day with lavish gifts, cards of greetings, flowers, and good wishes. In the evening a party is usually held, sometimes with dancing.

The climax of the evening comes when the honored birthday girl or young man is given the key to the house by the father. This key is usually made of a big piece of silver cardboard. It symbolizes the fact that, at twenty-one years of age, a person has reached the time of life when he is old enough to

have his own key to the family home, and can then come and go as he likes without first asking permission of his parents.

When the key is presented with great ceremony and fun, the new twenty-one-year-old will sing this traditional birthday song:

> *I'm 21 today, I'm 21 today,*
> *I've got the key of the door,*
> *Never been 21 before;*
> *Father says I can do as I like,*
> *So shout hip, hip, hooray,*
> *For he's a jolly good fellow,*
> *And I'm 21 today!*

After this important twenty-first birthday has passed, the British continue to enjoy celebrating their birthdays. British children always make a great thing of their parents' birthdays, although they try to be careful not to remind their parents of their age. Birthday cakes are always provided with the name in icing on top, but candles are left off, once the twenty-first birthday is past.

Should a person live to be eighty or more, the British make a greater fuss than ever over the birthdays. And should a person be lucky enough to reach the good old age of one hundred years, he is made happy by a telegram of congratulation from the Queen or the King.

In Greece

Children who live in the beautiful old country of Greece usually celebrate name days instead of birthdays; sometimes they celebrate birthdays, too.

Almost every day in the year is sacred to some saint in Greece, so name-day celebrations are everyday occurrences. Special church services begin the name-day observances. St. George's Day and St. John's Day attract the biggest crowds at church, because those are the most popular names in Greece.

During the name-day service, the priest talks about the saint whose day it is, and asks a blessing for all those who are celebrating in his honor.

When attending the church services, children whose name days are being celebrated like to wear the new clothes they have been given.

After the services are over, relatives and friends call throughout the day at the home of the one who is celebrating his name day. They usually bring some gift—candy, flowers, a toy, a book, or some article of clothing—whatever they think the person will like. The mother makes her guests welcome, and all enjoy visiting together. During the visit, choice treats are served the callers. Sometimes the mother serves *baklava,* a rich almond pastry; or *melopitta,* a sweet honey pie; or *karydopitta,* a delicious honey and walnut pie.

If friends live too far away to make a name-day call, they often send greeting cards, which carry the message, *Chronia Polla,* the Greek way of saying "Many happy returns of the day." They may choose, instead, to send telegrams of good wishes, or to telephone.

Sometimes it may not be convenient for those who are to celebrate their name days to keep open house. There may be illness in the family, or the person may be planning to be out of town on his name day, or he may simply not find it easy to entertain on that date. He will then have a notice published in the daily papers announcing that no open house will be held. Often long columns of such notices will appear in the paper, and relatives and friends respect these wishes.

On a child's name day, his mother often likes to serve a special dinner in his honor for the family. The dinner usually begins with soup—egg rice soup with lemon being one of the favorite kinds. This is followed by lamb, roasted in the same pan with potatoes and rice, or the lamb may be barbecued.

Some kind of Greek salad is almost always a part of the dinner, as is Greek cheese, called *feta*. Rice pudding is often the dessert. The meal ends with any fresh fruit in season—apples, melons, grapes, peaches, pears, or figs. Fruit is plentiful and delicious in Greece, and is relished by everyone. Black coffee is served at the end of the meal for those who want it.

When the parents wish to, they often give a party in the afternoon of their child's name day or on the birthday, whichever is being celebrated. Many Greek boys and girls prefer their own delicious Greek cookies and pastries to a birthday cake.

Ice cream is a special treat. Whenever it is served, the children all agree that it is tops!

A holiday is declared when the Greek King's name day arrives. Government offices all over Greece are closed for the day. In the morning of his name day, the King attends his name-day service in the Cathedral. He is accompanied there by a procession of high government officials—the President of the Parliament, the Prime Minister, cabinet members, the Supreme Court, the heads of churches in Greece, and all foreign ambassadors and ministers.

After the formal services at the Cathedral are over, all who attended go to the palace. Congratulations are offered to the King, and refreshments are served.

The Greek King thus sets the pattern for Greek name-day celebrations, which have become the custom in the villages, the cities, and in the country districts throughout the land.

feta—*feh*-tah

baklava—bahk-lah-*vah*

melopitta—mee-*loh*-pee-tah

karydopitta—kah-ree-*thoh*-pee-tah

Chronia Polla—*hroh*-nee-ah poh-*lah*

In Hawaii

Hawaii, our fiftieth state, is often spoken of as the "Paradise of the Pacific." Life is pleasant in those islands, where flowers bloom in profusion, and where the climate is as "heavenly" as it should be in a paradise. Hawaiians have always been friendly and fun-loving. They enjoy being together, singing old Hawaiian songs, dancing to the rhythmic music of native instruments, and feasting together at a *pa'ina* (old Hawaiian word for dinner party).

From earliest times, birthdays have served as one more excuse for the Hawaiians to come together. Ways of celebrating have changed through the years, but the enjoyment of them is the same.

The custom of celebrating birthdays goes back to those early peoples who, hundreds of years ago, found their way in canoes across the wide waters of the Pacific Ocean to establish new homes in the Hawaiian Islands. Among those first peoples, birthdays were celebrated only by the *ali'i* or chief's class. And even among the *ali'i*, a birthday celebration was a privilege granted only to the first-born son.

These very earliest birthday observances were always religious ones, and the feasting went on for days. The tribal priest, or *kahuna*, dictated the way the birthday was to be celebrated, and the ritual that was to be followed by the people. The *kahuna*, in turn, was guided by a seer or prophet, who would decide the kinds of gifts that should be presented to the first-born. The seer was supposed to have the power to foretell the future of the child, and woe be to anyone who dared to dispute his predictions! His judgment was final when it was put into effect by the *kahuna*. For instance, a seer might predict that the child would grow up to be a warrior, or a musician, or a dancer. The gifts that the *kahuna* would order to be presented would then be those that would be in keeping with the predicted future of the child.

With the coming of the American missionaries to the Hawaiian Islands over one hundred years ago, many of these old customs began to fade away. No longer were birthday celebrations limited to the first born of the *ali'i*, nor were *kahunas* and seers all-powerful in predicting futures and ordering gifts.

Today birthday parties are held by all who want to celebrate, and gifts are presented according to the wishes and the means of the givers. Feasting and merrymaking are enjoyed among all classes of people, although the old Hawaiian word for feasting, *pa'ina*, is no longer used by today's Hawaiians. This word was changed in 1856 to *lu'au*—the word for taro tops, which are always served at a feast.

Today a family may send out invitations to a birthday *lu'au* although, according to tradition, a birthday celebration does not require an invitation. Everyone is welcome to attend the party. It is understood, however, by all Hawaiians that a birthday donation is necessary for admission to the feast. This may be money or a present.

A large calabash—which is a bowl made of native wood, such as koa, milo, or monkey pod—is usually placed at the doorway of the house where the *lu'au* is to be held. As the guests enter the house, they greet the mother and father, and wish *Hauoli La Hanau* (Happy Birthday in Hawaiian way) to the child who is celebrating; then they place their gifts in the calabash. Many families save the money gifts for the child's education, but sometimes ex-

penses connected with the *lu'au* are paid first. Whatever is left is used as the parents see fit.

A birthday *lu'au* is often an elaborate affair.

The main part of the meal may be roast pork, baked in old Hawaiian fashion. A young fat pig is scrubbed and cleaned, then stuffed with hot lava stones, wrapped in a blanket of broad, long leaves from the ti-plant—a native shrub that grows everywhere in the islands—and laid on a bed of hot coals. The whole thing is covered with dirt and allowed to bake in its underground oven for many hours. When it comes out, the meat is tender and juicy. *Poi*, made from the taro plant, is always served with the roast pork, along with other Hawaiian delicacies—sweet potatoes, raw fish, kelp from the ocean, bananas, breadfruit, papaya, coconut milk, and pineapple juice.

Often at a *lu'au* the guests sit on the ground, picnic style, where the food is spread out in front of them on a long cloth covered with flowers of every color. Songs and dancing continue long after the feasting is over.

---

pa'ina—pah-*ee*-nah   ali'i—ah-*lee*-ee

kahuna—kah-*hoo*-nah   lu'au—loo-*ow*

Hauoli La Hanau—hah-oo-*oh*-lee lah hah-*nah*-oo

ti-plant—tee-plant   poi—poy

koa—*koh*-ah   milo—*mee*-loh

In Iceland

Until recently, birthdays were not observed in Iceland with any festivities. The most highly prized remembrances of the day were simple verses written by relatives or friends in honor of the one having a birthday. Among the many such verses are these, written for the birthdays of two little Icelandic girls:

> *Little girl with golden hair,*
> *May God your pathway smooth,*
> *Completed now is the fourth year*
> *Of your happy youth.*

and:

> *Few yet the friends you have, my dear,*
> *Except father, sister, mother;*
> *But they wish you happiness and cheer,*
> *As does your little brother.*

Since World War II, however, birthday celebrations have become much more common in Iceland. The celebrations are similar to those observed

in the United States, with parties, cakes, and candles. Refreshments, which are usually served at these birthday parties, include hot chocolate and pastries, such as *pönnukökur* (large thin pancakes folded in quarters and filled with jelly or jam and whipped cream) and *kleinur* (small oblong fried cakes).

Gifts that the birthday child has especially asked for are presented. When the gifts are offered, the guests at the party all wish him *Til hamingju med afmaelid*, which is the Icelandic way of saying "Happy Birthday."

Special celebrations are held when people reach their fiftieth, sixtieth, seventieth, and eightieth anniversaries, for older people are held in great respect by everyone in Iceland.

pönnukökur—*pooen*-noo-koo-kooer

kleinur—*klay*-noor

Til hamingju med afmaelid—teel *hahm*-ing-gue med

afv-myeh-leed

In India

If you were a Hindu child living in the great land of India, and were having a birthday, you would expect to have the celebration begin early in the morning, perhaps even before sunrise. From the time you awakened, to the end of the day, you would be the center of attention. It is the Hindu custom to make much of children's birthdays until they are sixteen years old. After that, young people are considered too old for celebrations.

A Hindu child gets up on his birthday as early as five or five-thirty in the morning. It does not take him long to bathe and dress in his best clothes. Sometimes he has new clothes to put on, given him by his parents as a birthday present.

As soon as he is dressed, he hurries first to his father to ask for his birthday blessing, and then to his mother for her blessing. When he has received their blessings, the Hindu child goes to the pictures of the Hindu gods which, according to custom, hang on the walls of every Hindu home. He then says a prayer and sings this song:

This is my birthday,
I am the creation of the Almighty,
Give me energy and wisdom
To serve my friends and parents.

I wish to do all my work
According to the will of God;
Help me not to cheat, not to speak untruths,
To honor the elderly, to serve others.

Guide me in proper ways
So that I may live
A long, happy life,
For this is my birthday.

Then, before he has breakfast, a Hindu child goes with his parents to take flowers to the temple and to pray. He rings the temple bells and the priest comes to hear the prayers. The child kneels low before the priest with his head touching the ground. When he finishes his prayers and lifts his head, the priest puts a red or black dye mark on the middle of his forehead to show that his prayers for a birthday blessing will be answered. The priest then gives him a sweet.

After the visit to the temple, the family returns home for breakfast. They find the house filled with excitement. All the uncles, aunts, cousins, and grandparents are hurrying about to get ready for the birthday celebration. Everyone is happy.

On this day, the Hindu child does not have to go to school, for Hindus believe that a special day such as a birthday is meant for prayer and for celebration. All day long everyone tries his best to give the child a happy day. No one speaks a cross word to him, for that would spoil his happiness. Instead, everyone tries to praise him and to make him feel good inside.

At noontime a birthday dinner is given for the cousins and special friends. The children sit on rugs on the floor in two rows facing each other. Low wooden trays, containing brass dishes that hold the birthday child's favorite foods, are placed on a pile of two pillows in front of each child.

Sometimes there is a spicy lamb curry, or a

curry made of potatoes and peas. *Dhal,* made of dried lentils, rice, and snowy white curds, may be served with the curry; or *chappaties,* round flat wheat cakes; or chutney, a peppery fruit relish. For dessert, a big tray of tempting fruits may be passed to the children—mangoes, apples, bananas—and as a special treat, a plate of fancy cakes.

After the dinner, the guests present their gifts—beads, bracelets, purses, scarves, or new records. The children like to listen to the new records and sing together before going into the garden to play games.

Sometimes, if the child is a girl, her mother may sing this birthday song to her:

> *Daughter, today you are queen of the stars,*
> *Everything in the world is happy for you*
> *Because today is your birthday.*

> *The moon is a small toy just for you,*
> *And all the flowers are smiling, too,*
> *Because today is your birthday.*

> *My own wish for you, my Daughter, is that*
> *All your life long you may be happy,*
> *Because today is your birthday.*

---

dhal—dahl

chappaties—chah-*pah*-tees

In Iran

Modern, oil-rich Iran, known until 1935 as Persia, lies between the Caspian Sea and the Persian Gulf. It forms a great land bridge in the Middle East, connecting Asia and Europe. Iran's matchless heritage, covering a span of twenty-five centuries, is a source of great pride to its twenty million people. They take pride, also, in the advances their country has made from an absolute monarchy toward the democracy it is building today.

They give much of the credit to their popular Shahanshah, Mohammad Reza Shah Pahlavi, for what has been done to establish schools and hospitals, and to improve living conditions.

The Shah's birthday, on October 26, is celebrated all over Iran as a national holiday. It is a time for rejoicing and merriment. Long birthday parades wind through the streets of the cities in the Shah's honor. In the evening, elaborate displays of fireworks light the skies in showers of stars and flaming balls of bursting colors.

During the day, people can be heard singing Iran's national anthem, which glorifies their Shah:

May our Sovereign live long and
The land under his rule be everlasting,
For, under Pahlavi came glory to the land
Far greater than time immemorial.
Threatened by her enemies,
The country found peace in his reign.
Happy are the people of Iran.
May the Almighty protect their Sovereign!

Iran is a Moslem country, over 97 per cent of the people following the religion that honors the prophet Mohammed. As in all Moslem countries, the birth of a son in Iran brings more joy than does that of a girl. One of the reasons for this is that the Iranians believe that marriage will take the daughter away from her family, while a son will look after his parents when he is grown. So the arrival of a boy is the occasion for great rejoicing. Wealthy families celebrate the event with music, dances, and feasting.

In some sections of the country, when either a boy or a girl is born, parents send out invitations for a dinner. If the new baby is a boy, rice with milk is served; if a girl, a kind of sugared omelet. With these special dishes, the parents may also provide caviar, especially if they live near the Caspian Sea, where caviar is produced in abundance, or *maast* (a form of yoghurt), or *chelo kabab* (a tasty dish made of grilled lamb, fluffy rice, and spices), with crisp raw vegetables as a side dish. The dinner usually ends with a light fruit sherbet. (Incidentally, the word "sherbet" comes from the Persian word *sharbat*.)

When the baby is seven days old, according to one of the ancient practices, he is given a name, in a ceremony called *Shab be-khair* (Good Night). The baby's father gathers his family, his close friends, and a few mullahs (priests). He serves them various sweets, and then the baby is brought in and placed next to one of the mullahs. The father writes five names for the baby on five separate pieces of paper. The papers are put into different pages of the Koran (the Mohammedan bible), or under a rug.

The first chapter of the Koran is recited, after which the father draws out one piece of paper at random, and the child is given that name. One of the mullahs whispers the name in the baby's ear, and slips the paper into his swaddling clothes. Friends then present money or other gifts to the new baby.

As children in Iran grow older, their birthdays are celebrated much as children in other countries celebrate theirs. They play games at an afternoon birthday party, and are served sandwiches and fruit drinks.

But the gifts are usually presented differently. Iranian boys and girls think it is a lot of fun to have a Treasure Hunt. When each guest arrives for the party he hides his gift in a secret place in the house or out in the garden. Then when the time comes for the Treasure Hunt, the birthday child goes in search of his presents. The other children laugh and shriek as they follow him from hiding place to hiding place until he has found them all.

The fun ends by everyone singing "Happy Birthday to You"—*Tavallode Shoma Mobarak Bashad*—in their Farsi language.

Shahanshah—Shah-an-*shah*

Mohammad Reza Shah Pahlavi—Moh-hahm-*mahd* Ray-*zah* Shah Pah-lah-*vee*

maast—mahst

chelo kabab—cheh-*loh* kay-*bahb*

sharbat—shahr-*baht*

shab be-khair—shahb beh-*kare*

mullah—moohl-*lah*

tavallode shoma mobarak bashad—tah-vah-loh-*deh* shoh-*mah* moh-bahr-*ahk* bah-*shahd*

In Israel

Israel is a young country. It celebrated its thirteenth birthday, or its "coming of age" anniversary in 1961. It chose this anniversary for special celebration because the thirteenth birthday is the birthday that every Jewish boy looks forward to as being the most important growing-up day in his life. To him and his family, it is also the most solemn day.

A Jewish boy's thirteenth birthday is known as *Bar Mitzvah.* At that time he becomes responsible for himself before God and his fellow men. The words *Bar Mitzvah* come from the Hebrew, and mean Son of the Commandment, or Son of the Law. The Law is the law of the Jewish people, called the *Torah.* The *Torah* is made up of the first five books of the Old Testament, which is their bible. When a boy becomes *Bar Mitzvah*, he accepts the *Torah*, and promises to live up to its laws. He thus becomes a "Son of the Law."

A boy's *Bar Mitzvah* is not celebrated on the actual day of his thirteenth birthday, but on the Sabbath (Saturday) nearest that date, as reckoned by the Hebrew calendar.

At least six months before his thirteenth birthday, a Jewish boy begins to study hard for his *Bar Mitzvah*, when he will go to the synagogue to appear before the rabbi, his family, and his friends. He wants his family to be proud of the way he has learned his lessons, so he studies very hard.

When the *Bar Mitzvah* Sabbath comes, the boy dresses in new clothes bought especially for the occasion, and goes to the synagogue with his father and mother. He takes his place on the pulpit, repeats the Hebrew blessings, then reads, in Hebrew, from the scroll of the *Torah*, that part of the scripture to be read on that particular Sabbath. After the reading, the boy gives a short talk before the congregation. He explains what the *Bar Mitzvah* ceremony means to him. He then discusses the chapter he has read from the *Torah*, and thanks his parents, his family, and his friends for all they have done for him during his thirteen years of growing up. He also thanks his teachers and the rabbis for their help in preparing him for his *Bar Mitzvah*.

After the service at the synagogue, the relatives and friends go with the boy and his parents to their home. He is showered with gifts—pens, pencils, wallets, key chains, books, briefcases, articles of clothing, or money. The guests like to show the boy how proud they are of him and of the way he took part in his *Bar Mitzvah*. They want him to know, too, how pleased they are that he is thirteen years old and a Son of the Law.

Even if there is no big party, there is almost always a *Bar Mitzvah* dinner for those who attended the ceremony. All have a happy time, but it is not hard to suppose that the happiest one of all is the thirteen-year-old *Bar Mitzvah* boy.

For thousands of years, among Jewish people round the world, the *Bar Mitzvah* ceremony was ob-

served for boys only. In modern times, girls go through a similar ceremony when they become twelve years of age. The girls' celebration is called *Bat Mitzvah*. Usually the girls' ceremony does not have a religious motive as the boys' has.

Small children in Israel celebrate their birthdays with a party much like those in the United States. A birthday cake is lighted with candles, and candies are served with it. When the children present their gifts, they like to sing this birthday song:

> *(Name) has a birthday,*
> *All the children are happy;*
> *(Name) has a birthday,*
> *And we all dance.*

Then the children place a crown of flowers on the birthday child's head and lead him to a special chair. When he is seated, several of the children take hold of the chair and lift him *up* and *up* and *up*, as many times as he is years old; then once more for the coming year. All the children laugh and clap as they lower the birthday child for the last time.

Bar Mitzvah—Bahr *Mitts*-vah

Bat Mitzvah—Baht *Mitts*-vah

Torah—*Toh*-rah

In Italy

Italy is made up of many different regions, each one having its own special kinds of foods, and its own traditional festivals. One custom that all parts of Italy have in common is the celebration of name days and birthdays, although the name day celebration is preferred in most parts of the country.

Name days in Italy are spoken of as *onomastico*, and the Happy Name Day greeting is *Buon Onomastico*. Birthdays are known as *compleanno*, and Happy Birthday is *Buon Compleanno*.

Name days and birthdays are anything but solemn occasions. They are happy family affairs, when relatives and friends are sometimes asked to join in the festivities.

Usually a name day begins with attendance at mass in church, when the patron saint of the one who is celebrating is honored. Later in the day comes the family dinner, when gifts are presented, and fancy cakes of all kinds are served.

Children who live in the great city of Rome

usually follow the custom of celebrating name days, because most Romans are named for saints. It is the general custom in Rome to hold an all-day open house on a name day. Friends may call at any time they wish to congratulate the one who is celebrating, and to leave a gift for him.

Some time during the day—at noon or at night —a grand dinner is served, which lasts for hours. Many fancy dishes, and many courses, make the meal a time of special pleasure for the relatives and friends who have been invited. On a Roman banquet table would probably be served such delicacies as: tender roast milk-fed lamb or roast suckling pig, fried artichokes, spaghetti, macaroni with sheep's cheese, and *gnocchi* (a delicious pasta made of flour and eggs). A variety of tempting fruits and cakes usually ends the feast.

Today, the American custom of observing birthdays for children is becoming more and more popular.

onomastico—oh-noh-*mahs*-tee-coh

buon onomastico—boo-*ohn*

compleanno—cohm-play-*ahn*-noh

gnocchi—*gnoh*-kee

In Japan

Japan is a land of festivals. Every month in the year brings its round of gay times, and children have their own special festivals to look forward to.

The Girls' Doll Festival is on the third of March. Girls dress in their best kimonos and bring out their special sets of dolls, which have been packed away all year. The dolls are displayed on shelves that look like steps. Then the girls invite their friends to their homes and they "play house."

Boys' Festival comes on the fifth of May. On this occasion, great floating carp, symbolic of courage, are flown from a long pole in the garden of every home having boys in the family. This festival, like so many Japanese customs, has changed in recent years, so that the day now is celebrated not for boys alone but for all children, and is called Children's Day.

Birthdays, too, come in for their fair share of celebrating. Buddha's Birthday Festival (the Flower

Festival) is celebrated on April 8. Boys and girls enjoy going to the temples that day to sprinkle the statues of the child Buddha with sweet tea as an expression of devotion, or just for the pleasure it gives them.

On November 15, the *Shichi-go-san* Birthday Festival is celebrated all over Japan, just as it has been for over four hundred years. *Shichi-go-san* means "Seven-Five-Three." On this day, girls of seven, boys of five, and all boys and girls of three dress in their best clothes, and go with their parents to the nearest Shinto shrine. There the parents give thanks to the gods for taking care of their children, and ask for their blessing. Sweets and paper talismans, which are supposed to bring them good luck, long life, and happiness, are often bought at the shrines for the children by their parents.

Children in Japan are always excited when a new baby arrives to join the family. They know that the birth of a new brother or sister will mean special celebations in which they will have a share.

According to the law in Japan, as soon as a baby is born, his name and the date of his birth are registered in the local government office.

When the baby is seven days old, he is the center of attention at the "Seventh Night" celebration.

His brothers and sisters join with other relatives and close friends to honor the baby's safe arrival.

The brothers and sisters do not have to wait long for the baby's first real festival. This takes place when a baby boy is thirty-two days old, or when a baby girl is thirty-three days old. According to the Japanese Shinto custom, this festival has some religious meaning.

The baby is dressed in his best clothes, usually made for this occasion by the grandmother on his mother's side. He is carried in his mother's arms in a procession that moves slowly toward the shrine. The older children follow and watch proudly as the Shinto priest blesses their baby and recites a sacred ritual.

After the shrine ceremony, the baby is taken to visit friends and relatives. They give him toy dogs, which symbolize their hope that he will grow as fast and be as healthy as a puppy! When the visiting is over, the brothers and sisters follow the procession to their home where a special feast is waiting.

The next birthday festival for the baby comes when he is about three months old. At this time, the other children help their mother as she prepares a small lacquer tray, on which she sets tiny bowls and dishes as symbols of the baby's first feast. The tray is arranged as shown on the next page.

1. rice bowl; 2. soup bowl; 3. fish dish; 4. dish for cooked vegetables; 5. pickle dish; 6. chopsticks

Sometimes the mother places a stone in one of the dishes as a wish that the child may have strong teeth. The children then help her as she sets the little tray in front of their baby, although they know that he will be given only one grain of rice to eat. The reason for this, of course, is that he is far too young for anything but milk.

When the baby is one year old, his brothers and sisters are ready to help him celebrate again! This time friends and relatives come to the baby's home to eat a special dinner in his honor. They offer a toast to his happy future as they sip their *sake* wine.

In the rural areas, a kind of fortune-telling ceremony is followed, similar to that in China and other Oriental countries. Various objects are spread around the baby, and the one he touches first is believed to foretell his future. This custom, however, has almost disappeared in the cities.

Until the end of the last war, in 1945, little attention was paid to children's birthdays after the third year. This was because the whole nation celebrated a common birthday at New Year's. On this day, as in China, everyone in Japan added a year to his age at the same time, and a double celebration was held. New Year's Day, celebrated on January 1, is the happiest festival of all. Special decorations are put up, inside and outside, and special foods are served.

Today in Japan, the custom of adding a year to everyone's age on New Year's Day is gradually giving place to the celebrating of individual birthdays. As the children learn more about the countries of the West, more and more of them are celebrating their birthdays "western style."

Buddha—*Boo*-dah

Shichi-go-san—shee-chee-*goh*-sahn

sake—*sah*-kee

In Korea

Korea, occupying a peninsula that points south from the eastern coast of Asia, is a little larger than the state of Utah. Korean children like to tell about their country's long history, which goes back to 2300 B.C., and about their ancestors who were the first people of the Far East to find a simple way of writing words, and the first to invent a movable metal printing type.

Many of the customs followed by Korean children, including the way they mark birthdays, show the influence of the Chinese, the Japanese, and, more recently, of the Western nations.

The birthday dinner is the central point of their birthday celebrations, when special foods are served that are not offered at any other time. The birthday child and the various members of his family sit on mats on the floor while they enjoy these specially prepared birthday dishes. One of their favorite dishes, which the Korean children think is a great treat, is sea urchin soup. The dinner ends with tasty rice cakes, made of ground rice powder. These are

baked in large enough quantities so that the children may eat them between meals for several days following the birthday dinner.

A baby's first birthday is celebrated with great ceremony. The same sort of custom that is followed in other Oriental countries is observed in Korea. The mother and father lay all kinds of articles on a table—pencils, pieces of money, books, and strips of cloth. The baby is then set down in the middle, and whatever the baby reaches for first is supposed to show what his future skills will be.

To the Koreans, the most important celebration of all comes when the "Papa-san," as the older man of the family is affectionately called, reaches his sixtieth birthday. At that time the entire family tries to have a reunion in his honor, when, with their friends, they mark the date with an elaborate feast.

In Mexico

In Mexico—that fascinating land to the south of the United States—it is the custom to begin a saint's day celebation early in the morning, the earlier the better! The fun may even start at midnight, just when the hands of the clock are beginning a new day, for it is the belief in Mexico that greetings and good wishes must be delivered as early as possible if the person is to have all the good luck that is wished. What is more, the greetings must be sung, much as our singing telegrams are. Is it surprising then that often these Mexican greetings serve as an alarm clock on the saint's day?

Mexican saint's day songs are called *mañanitas* and the singers are known as *mariachis*. *Mariachis* are strolling folk singers who are hired by relatives or friends to sing in front of the home of the one who is celebrating his saint's day. Early in the morning the *mariachis* come down the street with their musical instruments—guitars, violins, marimbas, horns, or cornets—and the haunting serenade begins.

After the *mariachis* have succeeded in waking everyone in the house, they are invited inside. There they are given a hearty breakfast of *frijoles* (Mexican beans), *tamales* (meat and cornmeal mush rolled in corn husks), *tortillas* (flat cornmeal cakes), and plenty of hot coffee.

Neighbors along the street, who have been awakened by the rousing songs, soon come dropping in to share in the food, to offer their good wishes, and to listen to the *mariachis* sing their *mañanitas*.

Of the many beautiful *mañanitas*, these two are among the most popular in Mexico:

EL DIA DE TU SANTO
Dios bendiga este día venturoso
y bendiga a la prenda que adoro
ya los angeles cantan en coro
por los anos que cumples, mi bien.

Las estrellas se visten de gala,
y la luna se llena de encanto
al saber que hoy es dia de tu santo
por los anos que cumples, mi bien.

THE DAY OF YOUR SAINT
May God bless you this day of fortune,
May He bless you, the one I adore.
All the angels in chorus now are singing,
For they know my love fulfilled another year.

All the stars up in heaven are shining,
And the moon radiates all its glory;
For they know it's the day of your Saint,
And that you, my love, fulfilled another year.

LAS MAÑANITAS DEL REY DAVID

Estas son las mañanitas
que cantaba el Rey David,
pero no eran tan bonitas
como las cantan aquí.

Despierta, mi bien, despierta
mira que ya amanecio';
ya los pajarillos cantan
la luna ya se metio'.

Si el sereno de la esquina
me quisiera hacer fav or,
de apagar su linternita,
mientras que pasa me amor.

THE MORNING SONG OF KING DAVID

With a morning song we greet you
As King David used to sing,
But his song was not as lovely
As is the music we bring.

Awake, then, oh my beloved,
Awake, for the dawn is nigh;
Now the birds are sweetly singing,
The moon has gone from the sky.

> *If the watchman at the corner*
> *Would be willing to comply,*
> *He would please put out his lantern*
> *The while my love's passing by.*

Mañanitas are really meant to be songs for grownups, especially for young ladies, although of course the whole family enjoys them.

Mexican boys and girls have their own fun on their saint's day. Sometimes they are given a special family dinner, although it is becoming more common for them to have a saint's day party similar to the birthday party in the United States. Whatever kind of party they have, they think it is not complete without a *piñata*. Breaking the *piñata* is the climax of any party.

The *piñata* is a wonderful creation, sometimes made by the grandmother or some other member of the child's family, sometimes bought at the market. The center of a *piñata* is a clay bowl of any size. Around this bowl is a covering of *papier mâché* (wet, pulpy paper), which is molded by hand into some kind of shape, and allowed to dry. It is then carefully covered with strips and strips of frilled paper in many colors, which are pasted into place. When the work is done, the *piñata* may look like some fantastic bird or other animal—a brightly feathered parrot, a gay rooster, a lamb, even *el toro*, the bull.

The inside of the jar is then filled with small

candies, nuts, or toys. The *piñata* is hung from a beam in the patio or from the ceiling inside the house.

When it comes time to break the *piñata* at the party, each child is blindfolded in turn and is given a big stick. Each child tries to strike the *piñata* hard enough to break the jar. Finally someone is lucky, and wham! the *piñata* breaks, and down comes a shower of goodies. All the *muchachos* (boys) and the *muchachas* (girls) scramble around on the floor until the last piece of candy and the last small toy have been picked up, so even if the *piñata* is broken before everyone has had his turn, all the children share in the scramble.

The most important birthday celebrated in a Mexican Catholic family is a girl's fifteenth birthday. On that day her parents present her to their friends at a reception or dance. The occasion is similar to the fifteenth birthday party in Brazil. The parents are proud of their daughter, dressed in a pale blue or pink silk party dress, with matching ribbons in her hair. This affair is their way of announcing that their daughter is now of marriageable age. You can see that Mexican girls marry at a much earlier age than girls do in this country, and that this party is similar to the coming-out parties or debuts in the United States.

mañanitas—mah-nya-*neet*-tahs

mariachis—mah-ree-*ah*-chees

frijoles—free-*hole*-es

tamales—tah-*mah*-lees

tortillas—tor-*tee*-yas

piñata—peen-*yah*-tah

papier mâché—pa-*pyay* mah-*shay*

muchachos—moo-*chah*-choes

muchachas—moo-*chah*-chas

el toro—ell *toh*-roh

In the Netherlands

In the Netherlands, once famous for its dikes and windmills, but now modern and highly industrialized, this is the birthday wish: *Lang zal hij (zij) leven!* In English these words mean: May he (she) live long!

The Dutch make a great deal of birthdays, for young and old.

Before Dutch boys and girls leave for school on the morning of their birthdays, the mothers fill their arms with biscuits, cookies, or candies for their classmates. The children give their teacher her share of the birthday treats, with perhaps an additional chocolate. In turn, the teacher presents them with an apple or a brightly colored card bearing her birthday greetings.

When school closes for the day, they hurry home to the birthday party their mother has prepared. Each guest brings a gift. First, games are played; then refreshments are served—all kinds of little cakes and cookies, and, of course, lollypops, which all Dutch children love.

The guests sing this happy birthday song to the birthday child:

> *Daar is er een jarig,*
> *Hoera, hoera,*
> *Je kunt het wel zien*
> *Dat is hij (zij)!*

> *There is someone having a birthday,*
> *Hooray, hooray,*
> *You can see that*
> *It is he (she)!*

While the children sing the last words, they point their fingers at the lucky boy or girl who is celebrating.

When the party is over, the birthday host gives a small gift to each of his guests. These gifts may be something like a pencil, a pencil sharpener, a packet of colored papers, a tablet, or a diary. Everyone receives a balloon, a paper hat, and some candies in a paper basket.

Summer birthday parties are often held out in a cherry orchard or in a berry garden. When it is time for refreshments, the children are allowed to eat all the fruit from the trees or bushes that their

stomachs can hold! No one stops them, but later some may wish they had not been so greedy!

As children grow older, their parties differ somewhat. There may be a puppet show, or a viewing of home movies that the father has taken. Teenagers prefer dinner parties at restaurants, or boating trips, or movie or theater parties.

One particularly interesting custom is often followed when a friend has been visiting in the home of a new acquaintance, if these new friends have found much in common and want to further the friendship. Before taking leave of his hostess, the visitor makes an excuse to examine a calendar, which hangs in one of the rooms of the house. The visitor is sure that he will find the birthday date of each member of the family marked on the calendar, because that is the custom in most Dutch homes. He quickly copies down the dates, slips the paper into his pocket, and returns to say good-by. He says nothing to his hostess about having copied the birthday information, but when the various dates come, he surprises everyone with a beautiful card, or a small remembrance. Thus the ties of friendship are forged more tightly, all because of birthdays!

Lang zal hij (zij) leven—Lahng zahl hay (zay) *lee*-ven

In Nigeria

Along the sandy beaches of the west coast of tropical Africa, in the curve of the map that looks like the inside of a giant "ear," lies one of the newest and most enterprising of Africa's independent countries. This country, known as the Federation of Nigeria, received its independence from Great Britain in 1960. It has a population of around forty million people, made up of three great groups— Yoruba, Ibo, and Hausa tribes—living in three regions of the country.

Many children among these three groups follow the old tribal custom of celebrating their birthdays as an age group, instead of having an individual birthday observance, although individual birthday celebrations are becoming more popular today.

The custom of having an age-group celebration began in very early times, when there was no calendar. The only way the people had of marking their birthdays was by the reign of a certain "king," or by some important event. People, then, who were born during one of these periods, became an age group, bound together by close life-long ties. They shared in each other's joys, sorrows, and successes. They celebrated their birthdays together.

According to the custom, when it was time for the age group to celebrate, one of the group agreed to act as host to the group. This custom is followed today.

The host may even choose the kind of material for the new clothes the members of the age group will wear for the celebration. This custom is followed by the Yorubas in particular. They call this birthday "uniform" *aso ebi.*

On the day chosen for the celebration, the preparation of the feast begins well before noon. While grownups are busy getting the food ready, the boys and girls of the age group get dressed in their *aso ebi,* and make themselves look their best.

Early in the afternoon, the dinner is ready. Children and adults sit down together, sometimes on mats under the trees, sometimes on the shaded verandas of their houses. They enjoy a delicious Nigerian stew, which is a birthday specialty. This stew is made of meat or fish, cooked with tomatoes and other vegetables, palm oil, red peppers, with salt and onion for seasoning. Rice is usually served with the stew, because it is the most popular food in all parts of Nigeria. Beans and other vegetables also go with the stew. In Yoruba, a delicacy called *fufu* is added to the birthday feast. *Fufu* is made of casava, which is similar to sweet potatoes.

After dinner, the children play games. "Hide-and-Seek" is one of their favorites, along with their

own native games—shell game (played something like jacks), pantomimes (played like charades), and clapping games.

When the children become tired of playing, some of the grownups may bring out their drums and start their thump, thump for dancing. The fun then really begins as young and old sway to the beat of the music.

Suddenly, the dancing may stop, as someone starts to chant. Everyone soon joins in the singing. Besides their native songs, Nigerian children especially like to sing "Happy Birthday to You," either in English or in their own language: *E̩ ku o̩dun O̩jo̩-ibi.*

Since their country's independence, boys and girls in Nigeria are especially proud to be singing their new Nigerian national song, not only at birthday celebrations, but on many other occasions.

Nigeria, we hail thee,
Our own dear native land,
Though tribe and tongue may differ,
In brotherhood we stand,
Nigerians all, and proud to serve
Our Sovereign Motherland.

Our flag shall be a symbol
That truth and justice reign,
In peace or battle honored,

And this we count as gain,
To hand on to our children,
A banner without stain.

O God of all creation,
Grant this our one request,
Help us to build a nation
Where no man is oppressed,
And so with peace and plenty
Nigeria may be blessed.

Whether boys and girls in Nigeria celebrate as an age group or have individual birthday celebrations, according to the new ways they have been learning about, they know how important each anniversary is, because young people are needed to take their places in their new nation.

~~~~~~

Yoruba—Yoh-roo-*bah*

Ibo—*Ee*-boh

Hausa—*How*-sah

aso ebi—aw-*sho eh*-bee

fufu—foo-foo

E ku odun Ojo-ibi—Eh koo aw-*dun* Ow-*jow-ee*-bee

In the Philippines

Boys and girls who live in the Republic of the Philippines, across the Pacific Ocean, sometimes celebrate on their own birthdays, and sometimes on their saints' days, if their families are Catholic. Whenever the families can afford it, children may be lucky enough to celebrate both anniversaries.

Saint's Day is usually observed by the parents taking the child to church the first thing in the morning. If at all possible, the parents provide new clothes for the child to wear on this occasion, because a new outfit is considered almost a *must* in the Philippines for this important service.

After the child has been to church and heard mass, he may go to his godparents to kiss their hands and to ask for their blessing. Pictures are then taken to record the milestone.

In the afternoon of the saint's day, and of the birthday, too, a dinner or a party is usually given for friends and relatives.

An old tradition is followed in many parts of

the Philippines of observing children's birthdays every seven years with a special celebration—on the first, the seventh, fourteenth, and twenty-first anniversaries. It is believed that these are the crucial years. If children can survive these seven-year hurdles successfully, then the parents think that they should be marked by special rejoicing.

An especially big feast is usually held on these occasions for members of the family and friends. Some kind of animal—a chicken, a pig, or even a cow, if the family can afford a cow—is prepared and roasted as the main part of this meal. Filipinos believe that the eating of meat on a birthday gives the birthday celebrant a new lease on life. Often the meat is roasted out-of-doors, especially in the country districts, on a hickory stick over a bed of coals.

Two native delicacies are usually served with the meat—tasty rice pastries, and a dish called *guinatan*, which is made of sweet potatoes, bananas,

jackfruit, and other tubers, cooked in coconut milk.

Children, as well as grownups, have a wonderful time at these seven-year birthday celebrations. They enjoy singing their own adaptation of the "Happy Birthday" song to honor the birthday child. Sung to the familiar tune, the words in Tagalog, which many Filipinos speak, are these:

> *Maligayang bati,*
> *Maligayang bati,*
> *Maligayang bati sa iyo,*
> *Maligayang bati mahal na (name).*

Gradually, the people in the Philippines are adopting American birthday customs. Children like ice cream and cake with candles at their parties, and have just as much fun with balloons, fancy caps, and all kinds of birthday favors as do boys and girls in the United States.

guinatan—gin-aah-*taan*

Maligayang bati—maah-li-*gah*-yang *bah*-tih

Tagalog—Tah-*gah*-log

In South Vietnam

In Southeast Asia, along the coast of the South China Sea, lies the country of South Vietnam. Children living there usually celebrate only two birthdays in their whole lives. Even then, they are too young to take much part in the celebrations, or to remember afterward what happened.

These two celebrations are held when a baby is one month old and when he is one year old.

It is the custom when the baby is one month old for the grandparents, close relatives, and friends to come to his house to see him. They offer prayers for his protection through life and beseech a blessing from the gods for a long and happy life.

Sometimes the guests bring small gifts for the baby—a jacket, a bonnet, a pair of shoes, or a soft toy.

The parents serve tea with cookies and cakes during the visits.

When a baby is one year old, a "cradle-leaving" celebration is held, even though he may continue to sleep in his cradle for a long time afterward. A better name for the celebration might be "mother's bedroom-leaving" day. On this first birthday, following the custom of Vietnam, a baby is considered old enough to be taken out of his mother's room, where he has been sleeping since he was born, and moved into the room with his brothers and sisters.

As on all other Vietnamese festivals, the birthday begins with a religious ceremony. Members of the family and friends gather around the parents and offer special foods to the gods as they pray for a blessing on the baby. Red-painted eggs and colorful cakes are served, with the usual rice.

After the offerings of food have been made to the gods, the baby is placed in the center of a table for his fortune telling, a custom similar to the one followed in China, Japan, and Korea.

All kinds of objects are placed around the baby —an egg, small cakes, a ruler, a piece of brightly colored cloth, or a book. Following the Oriental custom, the family gathers around to see which object the baby will reach for first, but a somewhat different meaning is given to the baby's choice.

If the child reaches for the egg first, he will *not* be a scholar. If he touches the cake first, he will not be bright in school, but will be shrewd in business. If he grabs the ruler, he will like perfection, but may be hot-tempered. If the baby handles the piece of cloth, he will be frivolous, but if he picks up the book, of course it is believed that he will grow up to be an "egghead"!

Naturally, it does not always work out this way, any more than it does in China or Japan or Korea, since this fortune-telling ceremony is only a superstition. Many Vietnamese babies grow up to be just the opposite of what their one-year-old choices indicated they would be.

What is more important to the Vietnamese than the celebration of these two birthdays is their custom of marking the anniversaries of the days when beloved members of the family have gone to join their ancestors.

These "death anniversaries," as they are called, are not sad times of mourning for, according to the Buddhist beliefs which the Vietnamese follow, there is no such word as "die." They believe that those who are no longer living on earth have simply finished the life here, and have gone on into a new and better life. By keeping "death anniversaries," they believe they are not only honoring the departed, but are giving their children an opportunity to be reminded of the respect they owe to those who have gone on before.

"Death anniversaries" are held for each member of the family who has departed, as far back as the great-grandparents.

Sometimes, relatives and close friends will come long distances to join in the celebration. Often a Buddhist priest is invited to lead the family in prayers for the souls of those who have gone on to a better life. During the religious service, the members of the family offer food on the altar for the departed, and burn pieces of yellow paper to carry their blessings in the rising smoke to the souls of the dear ones.

After the religious service, the family and guests sit down to enjoy the feast together. This gives the housewife a chance to show her skill in cooking. She sets before her guests the finest variety of food she has been able to prepare—roast pork, perhaps, or meat and fish cooked in coconut milk, eggroll, and rice, without which a meal in Vietnam is not quite complete. For dessert, there may be cakes made of rice flour, or a variety of tropical fruits— bananas, oranges, grapefruit, mangoes, papayas.

Even though many childen in South Vietnam are now beginning to celebrate their birthdays much as the boys and girls in the United States do, their favorite celebrations are still the days when they honor those in their families who have gone.

~~~~~~

Xin thành thật chúc một sinh nhật dẩy hoan hỉ
Sin tahn   taht chook mote sin neuht day hwan hee
(Happy birthday in Vietnamese)

In Thailand

Thailand, known until recent times as Siam, is a fascinating country in southeastern Asia. It has a wealth of traditions, which are steeped in religious beliefs. The children have been brought up to worship Buddha as their god. Their religion, called Buddhism, is the religion of about 95 per cent of the people in Thailand. Buddhism plays an important part in the customs of the country, birthday celebrations included.

According to tradition, a birthday celebration begins on the eve of the anniversary. The exact hours for this pre-celebration and for the ones on the next day are set by a "reliable" fortune-teller. Children and grownups, too, are sure that the hours chosen by the fortune-teller will be those that will bring them good luck.

Before any celebration begins, elaborate preparations must be made. The house must be made spick and span, offerings for the Buddhist priests must be gotten ready, and the birthday candles must be obtained from a nearby store, if they are not made at home.

On the anniversary eve, a number of priests are invited to the ceremony to offer blessings, and to receive the special offerings provided by the one having a birthday. People who are particular about following the old traditions are careful to invite three more priests than they are years old.

The offerings for each priest are usually placed on a tray or in a tin pail, and include such things as rice, flowers, joss-sticks, tea, yellow robes, towels, or other articles that the priests will find useful.

An important part of this birthday-eve ceremony is the lighting of the two birthday candles that have been prepared for this occasion. The center of one of the large wax candles, which, preferably, has been homemade, contains thirty-two strands of special cotton, as long as the distance around the crown of the birthday person's head.

The other candle is the "personal candle." This is as tall as the height of the birthday person, from his feet to the top of his head. Once this "personal candle" is lit, great care is taken not to let it go out until the entire candle has burned down; if the flame blew out, that would mean bad luck.

Early on the next morning, the Buddhist priests, dressed in their saffron-yellow robes, each with an alms bowl, and possibly a big black umbrella held

over his head, start out on their rounds to have
their bowls filled with rice for the day. They do
this every day, but on a birthday morning, they
wait to be asked before visiting that home.

If a priest is among the invited ones, his alms
bowl will be filled to overflowing with rice and
vegetables.

Later, on the birthday morning, comes the
ceremony of the freeing of the animals. According
to tradition, if the parents of the child can afford it,
the father and mother buy as many birds or fish,
sometimes both, as their child is years old, plus one
extra animal for the child to "grow on."

After sprinkling each animal with blessed

water, the boy or girl lets the birds fly free, and returns the fish to the waters of the river or canal. This ceremony is believed to insure the favor of the gods for the coming year. It also symbolizes the old Buddhist belief that no one should ever do any evil thing to animal life. Depriving animals of their freedom is considered evil.

On the afternoon of the birthday, Thai children will probably enjoy a birthday party like that of the children in the United States. The Thai children like to present gifts, play games, and have refreshments. They are fast adopting the custom of a birthday cake with candles.

In the U.S.S.R.

Children's birthdays are celebrated as festive and happy occasions in Soviet families and Soviet schools.

In many families, the day begins in a happy way for the child as soon as he opens his eyes in the morning. On a table or chair beside his bed, or tucked under his pillow, he finds the gifts his family have put there for him while he was asleep. His mother and his father, and his brothers and sisters greet him with a cheery *S Dnyem Rozhdenya.*

During the day, children are reminded of the anniversary by members of their families, by their friends, their schoolmates, and their teachers. Gifts are presented, and everyone tries to do something kind for those who are celebrating and to make them realize the importance of the occasion. It is impressed upon them that during the next year they must try their best to be "healthy, happy, and wise."

There is usually a special holiday dinner or tea. Sweet pastry, fruit, cakes, candies—whatever the birthday child likes best—are served by his mother. She also likes to bake him a special birthday pie, which takes the place of a birthday cake for Soviet children. The pie is often apple or cherry, with the name of the child and the greeting, *S Dnyem Rozhdenya*, pricked on the crust before it is baked. The first piece of pie that is cut always goes to the one who is being honored.

Cards and letters of good wishes are received from relatives and friends who may live too far away to bring their greetings in person.

Often the parents plan a birthday party in the afternoon, when the school friends join the celebrating child in having fun dancing and playing games. One of the favorite singing games at birthday parties is *Karavai*, or "The Round Loaf."

> *On Tanya's birthday*
> *We bake a round loaf,*
> *So—wide,*
> *So—high,*
> *So—low,*
> *So—narrow.*
> *Round loaf, round loaf,*
> *Let him who wishes*
> *Take some.*
> *I love you all,*
> *But someone special more than all!*

The children join hands to form a circle around the birthday child. They move to the rhythm of the song, then show the dimensions of "The Round Loaf," first by making the circle as large as they can when they come to the words, "So—wide"; then by raising their joined hands above their heads for "So—high"; by squatting, for "So—low"; and by drawing the circle in toward the center, as they sing "So—narrow." This is the most exciting part of the game. The child in the center chooses someone from the circle to take his place; then he joins the circle, and the game continues.

When the games and dancing are over, the children all sit down while the father and mother make a ceremony of presenting their gifts. The parents tell their birthday child how proud they are of him, what he has meant to them during the past year, and how much they are expecting of him during the coming year.

While the child stands in the center of his group of friends, each guest offers congratulations and presents his gift. The gifts may include flowers, candy, sometimes tickets to the children's theater, a new dress or suit, a musical instrument, or a particular toy the child has wished for—perhaps a construction set, a game, doll, doll-house furniture, or toy dishes. The favorite gifts are always books, for books are prized possessions in the U.S.S.R.

Children look forward to going to school on their birthdays, because each one knows that some surprise is probably being planned for him by his

teacher and his classmates. It is the custom in the Soviet Union for a teacher to keep, in a special book, a record of the birthdays of the children in her class. When she sees that one of her pupils will shortly have a birthday, she will set up a committee of a few in the class to plan how they will mark the occasion.

Promptly at nine o'clock on the birthday morning, as soon as school begins for the day, the teacher will ask the one who is having a birthday to stand. Then, on behalf of the class, she gives him their congratulations and good wishes, and the committee presents some surprise, usually flowers.

Also, the pupils, on the birthday of one of their classmates, wear their school uniforms. These are worn only on special occasions, such as the first week of school, the week of November 7—which is the Soviet National Holiday—and the weeks of examinations—in May and June. If the birthday pupil is a girl, she will wear red, blue, or green bows on her braids to set off the uniform—a brown dress and white apron. The boys' school uniforms are navy blue suits.

Kindergarten children may be given small gifts by their teachers and friends during lunch time. Often these gifts have been handmade by the children.

The sixteenth birthday is a landmark in the lives of teenagers in the U.S.S.R., and is an occasion for special celebrations, usually with an evening party and dance. On this day all sixteen-year-olds are given internal passports by the government in recognition of their becoming adults.

The eighteenth birthday is an important one, too, because at eighteen Soviet young people are given the right to vote.

S Dnyem Rozhdenya—ssdihn-*yum rozh*-deh-nee-yah

Karavai—kah-rah-*vy*e

In Venezuela

Boys and girls living in the Republic of Venezuela are proud of their big country, which lies in the northern part of South America along the shores of the Caribbean Sea. They are proud, too, that Columbus discovered their country, and that from their Spanish ancestors, who came in the footsteps of Columbus, they inherited their language, their form of religion, and many of their customs.

One of these old Spanish customs is the celebration of Saint's Day. This day is regarded by every Venezuelan child, who has been given the name of a saint, as a special time for honoring his patron saint. Whenever a child does not have the name of a saint, then he celebrates his own birthday anniversary instead.

The favorite way to celebrate either day is to have a party. As the time draws near, the child who is about to celebrate becomes more and more excited. He thinks he can hardly wait for the big party he knows his mother is planning for him. He makes sure that all his friends are invited well in advance, and that everything is ready for the party.

Because the weather in Venezuela is generally warm, the parties are usually held in the garden. This gives the children a chance to play such games as *Hide and Seek; Ring, Ring, Who Has the Ring;* and other games similar to those you play at your birthday parties.

When each guest arrives at the party, he presents a gift to the honored child, who opens the wrappings excitedly and admires the toy or game or doll. He says *Gracias* (thanks) to the giver, while his mother very carefully writes down the name of the gift and the giver, so that later she can be sure of writing a note of thanks to the right person.

After the gifts have been enjoyed, the children join in singing Happy Birthday. Sometimes they like to sing the words in English, and sometimes they like to sing their own Spanish words:

> *Feliz cumpleaños para ti,*
> *Feliz cumpleaños para ti,*
> *Feliz cumpleaños para (name),*
> *Feliz cumpleaños para ti.*

The refreshment table is often set out under the trees. It is decorated with flowers and heaped high with plates of good things to eat. Each guest finds a small favor or toy at his place, which adds to

the fun. Usually the mother has prepared sandwiches, small sausages, cookies, and cakes. With
these, orange juice and cokes are served. Ice cream
completes the feast. With the ice cream, a lighted
birthday cake is brought in. Just as you do, the birthday child makes a wish and blows out the candles.

When refreshment time is over, the children
are ready and impatient for the crowning event of
the party—the breaking of the *piñata*. This event is
a must at birthday parties in Venezuela, just as it is
in Mexico, but the Venezuelan variety of *piñata* is
somewhat different.

Instead of using a clay jar for the inside of the
piñata, the Venezuelan *piñata* is formed entirely of
papier mâché. While the paper is moist, it is shaped
very carefully to represent some large figure, such
as a clown, a donkey, a monkey, a bird, a doll, or
sometimes an airplane. The inside of the *papier
mâché* is hollowed out to form a container which,
when dried, will be filled with candies, whistles,
tops, balls, or other small toys. When the paper
figure is dry, the outside is covered with brightly
colored paper, so that the object looks quite real
when it is finished.

All during the party, the *piñata* has been swing-
ing by a rope from the branch of a tree. The children
keep going over to look at it, for they know the fun
they will have when the time comes for them to try
to break it.

Finally, the time does come and they make a dash for the *piñata*, and form a big circle around it. Just as in Mexico, each child is blindfolded and given a stick with which he whacks away when his turn comes. To make his task harder, and to add more excitement for those who are watching, the father or the mother raises and lowers the rope to which the *piñata* is tied. Just as the blindfolded child is about to strike the *piñata*, the rope is raised so that the *piñata* is just out of his reach. Then it is quickly lowered again, and the fun starts over.

Finally a lucky child comes down with a big whack of his stick. The *piñata* breaks, and its hidden surprises scatter over the ground in all directions. The children laugh and shriek as they scramble after them. The quickest child of course gets the most!

After the *piñata* fun is over, the children begin to say their good-bys and start for home. At the door, the mother and the honored child hand each guest a special present such as a doll, toy automobile, small boat, box of crayons, or story book.

---

gracias—*grah*-cee-ahs

feliz cumpleaños para ti—feh-*lees* coom-play-*ahn*-yoes *pah*-rah tee

HAPPY BIRTHDAYS
ROUND THE WORLD

As you complete this imaginary birthday tour of twenty-four countries round the world and see how children celebrate their anniversaries, perhaps you begin to see how much alike children are everywhere. Like you, they regard birthdays as something quite special, whether they celebrate their own anniversaries, or the days held sacred to their saints, or even the "death anniversaries" of their ancestors, as they do in South Vietnam.

You see how they enjoy good times and have fun playing games at their parties; how they, too, enjoy birthday surprises, and think that refreshments make a birthday party. Like you, they enjoy singing their happy birthday songs and expressing their good wishes for "many happy returns of the day," even though the words they use may sometimes be strange-sounding.

Birthdays have a way of bringing children everywhere closer together. When you make a wish and blow out your birthday candles, the children in Germany seem to have much in common with you. You are grateful that the early settlers to this country brought their favorite birthday customs with them, so that you can enjoy them, too. In return, you are glad that you can share some of your customs with children of other lands. This is especially true of the way your American "Happy Birthday to You" song has really become international.

Getting to know more about children of other lands—what they like to do, what they are thinking—and sharing good things with them, help to create a friendly feeling toward them and an understanding of their way of life.

Gabriela Mistral, once poet laureate of Chile, wrote: "When the young people of all the nations of the world understand each other, then we shall indeed have peace on earth." We can only hope she was right.

ACKNOWLEDGMENTS

⸺For providing information on birthday customs, and for reviewing and approving the final manuscript, the author is sincerely grateful to: Marguerite Gilson, Brussels, Belgium; René Marenne, Embassy of Belgium; Florita Bellé, Embassy of Brazil; Catholic Information Center, Washington, D.C.; M. Nathan, Embassy of Ceylon; Punitham Tiruchelvam, Colombo, Ceylon; You Yu Bao, Embassy of the Republic of China; Florence Ho, Hong Kong; Gertrud Goldkuhle and Marie-Louise Roessler, Embassy of the Federal Republic of Germany; Jane Tsitsiwu, Washington, D.C.; William Tsitsiwu, Embassy of Ghana; Oliver Lambert, Truro, Cornwall, England; Pierre Calogeras, Myrto Liatis Denby, and Demetrios Georgantopoulos, Royal Greek Embassy; the Reverend Samuel A. Keala and Barbara W. Salvani, Honolulu, Hawaii; Ingvi S. Ingvarsson, Icelandic Embassy; Mekkin S. Perkins, Des Moines, Washington; Pushkar Johari, Embassy of India; Haridas R. Parekh, Bombay, India; Mrs. H. C. Singhal, New Delhi, India; Colonel Kai Rasmussen, Washington, D.C.; Farhad Sepahbody, Embassy of Iran; Aviva Grinberg, Embassy of Israel; Lucio Cecconi, Italian Embassy; Roberto Franceshi, Italian Information Center, New York City; Sachiko Hashimoto, Tokyo, Japan; H. Uyehara, Embassy of Japan; Sung Ho Lee, Korean Research and Information Office, Washington, D.C.; Mary R. Spencer, Albuquerque, New Mexico; Jenny Wells Vincent, Taos, New Mexico (for her kind permission to use her translation of the song, *El Dia De Tu Santo*); Dirk J. van Wynen, Embassy of the Netherlands; Aliyu Y. Bida and Bukunola Osibodu, Embassy of Nigeria; Wilma K. Miller, Ibadan, Nigeria; Consuelo Barte, Tacloban City, Philippines; Loreto Paras-Sulit, Manila, Philippines; Manuel A. Viray, Embassy of the Republic of the Philippines; Le this Bai, Voice of America; Blanche Cao, Saigon, South Vietnam; Laura Mayer, Bangkok, Thailand; Nadya Khimatch, Embassy of U.S.S.R.; Dina Perfilevskoya, Moscow; F. J. Lara, Embassy of Venezuela.

For assistance with pronunciations, the author is indebted to linguists, to nationals of the various countries, and to members of the embassies. (In some instances, it has been difficult to indicate exactly the pronunciation of certain foreign words, since there are no equivalent sounds in English. The pronunciations used are as close as it was possible to make them.)

The words of the song *Happy Birthday* on page 17 are Copyright by Summy-Birchard Company, Evanston, Illinois, and are used by permission.

For advice and assistance in the preparation of the material, the author is grateful to: Doris Ambrose, Irene Backus, Lena S. Bratter, Frances Cavanah, Agnes De Lano, Maurice Flagg, Helen Monegan, Frances Smith, and Mrs. Milton J. Stickles.

INDEX

PRINTED IN U.S.A.